FRANCESCO VALCANOVER

JACOPO TINTORETTO AND THE SCUOLA GRANDE OF SAN ROCCO

139 COLOUR PLATES

Cover Picture:
Christ before Pilate (detail)

STORTI EDIZIONI

The facade of the Scuola Grande di San Rocco.

THE SCUOLA GRANDE DI SAN ROCCO

The Scuola di San Rocco is certainly the best preserved, as regards the architecture and fittings, of Venice's six Scuole Grandi (Major Guilds) which for many centuries, together with the minor Confraternities, formed the thick network of brotherhoods of a religious nature. These were set up to help the poor and the sick, or to protect the interests of individual professions, or to help the weak and needy members of non-Venetian communities living in the city.

The guild dedicated to San Rocco of Montpellier who died in Piacenza in 1327 and whose remains are thought to have been brought to Venice in 1485, was legally recognized in 1478. Its aim was to relieve the suffering of the sick,

A View of Campo San Rocco.

3

especially those stricken by the epidemics. Initially its premises were situated near the church of San Giuliano. Later, after many vicissitudes, they were transferred close to the apses of the church of Santa Maria Gloriosa dei Frari. Here, during the years spanning the 15th and 16th centuries, the Scuoletta, used for meetings of the brothers, and the church of San Rocco were built according to a project by Bartolomeo Bon, overseer of San Marco and between 1765 and 1771 the facade was redone by Maccaruzzi. Soon the enormous economic resources, augmented by the offerings of those devoted to the venerated remains of St. Roch and to the miraculous image of "Cristo portacroce" (Christ carrying the cross) by Titian, made the Confraternity bank decide on the building of far more imposing premises which were to become

The rear facade of the Scuola Grande di San Rocco.

A. Scarpagnino, The great staircase in the Scuola Grande di San Rocco.

one of the most characteristic and fascinating examples of town planning in Venice: the Campo di San Rocco. The grandiose building, opposite the Scuoletta, was begun in 1517 by Bartolomeo Bon who designed it and supervised the work until 1524. Bon was succeeded for two years by Sante Lombardo because of disagreements with the clients. Work was suspended in 1526 only to be started again the following year, and it was finished in 1549, the basic part of it under the supervision of Antonio Abbondi called Scarpagnino. The finishing touches to the building lasted until 1560 under the direction of Giangiacomo dei Grigi. This imposing building shows a certain lack of architectural continuity due to the long time the work took because of the quarrels between work supervisors and clients. The plan of the building and the design of the lower part of the facade and of the side portico with its wide two-lighted mullions designed by Bartolomeo Bon, reflect the architectural trends of the end of the 15th and the beginning of the 16th centuries in Venice. Scarpagnino harmonised the lower part of the building with the remainder by means of a series of purely decorative 16th century columns. They are similar to the other pilasters which separate the twin windows with their triangular pediments on the upper part of the facade, which was probably never finished as it should have been. Scarpagnino was also responsible for the wide main entrance (1549) and the great staircase (1544) which joins the ground floor room to the upper one. All building work was finished in 1560 and four years later Jacopo Tintoretto began his pictorial decorations of the rooms. This work, which took him until 1588, constitutes one of the most fascinating pictorial undertakings ever known: from 1564 to 1567 the 27 canvases on the ceiling and walls of the Hall of the Hostel, where members of the Banca and Zonta, who governed the brotherhood, used to meet; from 1576 to 1581 the 25 canvases on the ceiling and walls of the Upper Hall; from 1582 to 1587 the eight large canvases in the Ground Floor Hall which in 1587 was adorned with the altar bearing the statue of St. Roch by Girolamo Campagna; in 1588 the altarpiece with a statue by Girolamo Campagna at each side. The altar had been erected the previous year in the Upper Hall. The decoration of the Scuola continued during the following centuries in as much as the already massive presence of Jacopo Tintoretto's work allowed. In 1656 Antonio Zanchi painted a majestic work on canvas on the right-hand wall of the staircase to commemorate the end of the plague in 1630 and then in 1673 Pietro Negri undertook the decoration of the oppostite wall. During the second half of the 17th century Francesco Pianta, the Younger, completed a series of twelve caryatids along the walls of the Upper Room opposite the staircase. These were sculptured in the baroque style and in obscurely bizarre ways. The sculptor himself explains their interpretation on the scroll of imitation parchment held in Mercury's hand to the right of the staircase, after having sculptured two figures near the altar, one being a cariacature of Jacopo Tintoretto and the other his own effigy in the act of unmasking himself. Then towards the end of the 17th century, Girolamo Pellegrini painted the fresco on the dome over the staircase landing while the 24 pieces of richly carved relief wood-work by Giovanni Marchiori are signed and dated 1743. These illustrate episodes from the life of St. Roch and show a polished elegance of rococo style as they decorate the presbytery walls of the Upper Room. This presbytery is closed off by a bronze gate cast in 1756 and designed by Giuseppe Filiberti. The pictorial decorations by Giuseppe Angeli

F. Pianta, the Younger, Portrait of Jacopo Tintoretto.

on the Chancery ceiling belong to 1754 and are arranged within the stucco-work by Carpofaro Mazzetti Tencolla. The last exacting piece of work in the Scuola dates back to 1885-90 when the floor of the upper room was relaid according to a design by Pietro Saccardo.

Immediately after the end of the Republic the Scuola, all the richer for paintings by Titian, by Strozzi and by Tiepolo, was included in the list of buildings subject to suppression under Napoleonic rule. This meant the loss of the enormous patrimony and of a part of the precious religious ornaments. Fortunately none of the paintings were lost and they soon came under the responsibility of a competent body when the Scuola was re-opened in 1808.

However the governors of the brotherhood had always seen to the preservation of the great pictorial display by Jacopo Tintoretto. Some of the restoration works can be dated exactly as the recent results of research in the archives shows (P. Rossi, The Work of Domenico Tintoretto, Sante Piatti and Giuseppe Angeli for the Scuola di San Rocco, in "Arte Veneta", 1977): by Domenico Tintoretto in 1602 ("Probatica piscina", cf. pag. 84); by Angelo Vidali in 1673 (the large canvases in the Hall of the Hostel, in 1674 ("The miracle of the loaves and fishes", cf. pag. 77), "The temptation of Christ", cf. pag. 81) and in 1678 "Assumption of the Virgin", cf. pag. 126); by Lelio Bonetti in 1696 ("Probatica piscina", cf. pag. 84); by Gaetano Zompini before 1672 (canvases in the Hall of the Hostel), After being chosen as restorer of the "numerous precious paintings of the Scuola" in 1770, the painter Giuseppe Angeli, from 1771 onwards, devoted himself to the demanding restoration work of the ceiling canvases in the Upper Room. He went over the original paintings, even redoing in oils the chiaroscuro tempera of Tintoretto's rhomboid forms. The last documented restoration work was carried out by Florian in 1834 ("Assumption of the Virgin", pag. 126).

At the end of the sixties a thorough restoration of all Tintoretto's paintings, except the canvases on the ceiling of the Hall of the Hostel, was undertaken. This was made necessary by the thick layer of dirt and non-original coats of varnish and above all the fact that the original canvases had been removed from their supports so compromising the stability of the colours. Financed mainly by Edgard J. Kaufman Charitable Foundation of Pittsburg through the Venice Committee of the American International Fund for Monuments and entrusted to Antonio Lazzarin by the Soprintendenza ai Beni Artistici e Storici di Venezia, the work was carried out between 1969 and 1974. During the restoration, which has enabled a more authentic interpretation of Tintoretto's masterpieces, it was possible to verify just how Tintoretto prepared himself to face painting the various themes by first making sketches on the canvas. In these large sketches of the final composition, visible too in photographs taken with infra-red rays, the figures are outlined in the nude, as they are in the few signed drawings of single figures by Tintoretto. The fact that the artist preferred to define his ideas on the finished whole by means of graphic notes directly on the canvas, clarifies his method of work and explains the almost total absence of preparatory drawings done on paper. Restoration work has also made it possible to explain how the general harmony of colour in the painting has notably darkened due to the alteration with time of some pigments and their relative colour combinations. In particular the blue has become lead-grey, the

J. Tintoretto, "Christ praying in the Garden", a detail photographed with infra-red rays.

green brown, the red pale pink, the yellow amaranth. This has created an irreversible change which, if on the one hand has lessened the tone-colour vividness of the chromatic harmony, on the other hand has increased that intensity of luministic effects which originally must have been dramatically set off in the semi-darkness of the rooms, especially in the Upper Room. It is necessary to take into account this change of colour when appraising Jacopo Tintoretto's paintings at the most important moments in the art of this great Venetian artist and in European painting in the second half of the 16th century.

JACOPO TINTORETTO
BEFORE HIS WORK
IN THE SCUOLA DI SAN ROCCO

Jacopo Robusti, called Tintoretto after the occupation of his father Giovanni Battista who was a dyer of silk materials, was born in Venice presumably in 1519 since his age when he died on 31 May 1594 was given as seventy five. Towards 1550 he married Faustina Episcopi, the daughter of Marco, Guardian Grande in 1547 of the Scuola di San Marco. They had several children including Marietta (1554 c.), Domenico (1560) and Marco (1561) who were also painters playing an active part in their father's organized workshop. Sources describe Tintoretto as being short and having a proud and obstinate character. In a document dated 1539, at just twenty years of age, he already seems to be an independent master. His developing years fall therefore in that very important period when the Venetian pictorial scene was undergoing renewal, pressed by the mannerist stimoli caused by the stay of Venetian artists in the centres of the new Roman, Tuscan and Emilian art which had sprung up following Raphael and Michelangelo; by the circulation of drawings and prints in that style in the Veneto; by the presence in Venice of Tuscan artists such as Jacopo Sansovino, Francesco Salviati and Giuseppe Porta, Giorgio Vasari. The first works of Tintoretto, who is said to have frequented for a very short time Titian's workshop, reflect this climate and are particularly rich in the influences of the creative ease of Bonifacio Veronese and Schiavone, the sophisticated elegance of Paris Bordone, the plastic-chiaroscuro strength of Pordenone, the overwhelming expressive vitality of Michelangelo. The young Venetian artist made the latter's sculpture, together with the classical, the object of frequent graphical copies. Tintoretto's language matured and had its first impressive achievements in the "Supper" of 1547 in the church of San Marcuola and in the "Miracle of St. Mark" painted in 1548 for the Scuola dedicated to the Saint of the same name and which today hangs in the Accademia Galleries. In these works some of the fundamental tones which characterize his style appear clearly asserted: the overwhelming and compositive vitality of the spatial-perspective creativity; the rapidity of the brush-work; the emphasis on three-dimensional modules and chiaroscuro outbursts of colour; the controlled capacity for gestures and poses; the impassioned force of locally important colours which change quickly in cold tones. In his portrayal of reality, narrative, spontaneous and harmonious, which immediately arouses the emotion of the onlooker, light increasingly becomes the main protagonist, in contrast to Titian's elegant stress on tonality. At the beginning of the sixth decade, in a series of masterpieces including the "Story of Genesis" for the Scuola della Trinità and today at the Accademia Galleries, the "Susanna and the Elders" in the Kunsthistorisches Museum in Vienna, the organ doors in the Venetian church of the Madonna dell'Orto, light keeps its primary role even when Tintoretto's creative strength, coinciding with the rapid rise in fortune of the glorious painting of Paolo Veonese, becomes more relaxed and takes on a calmer expression of figurative rhythms and cadences and a greater harmony of clear chromatic tones. Soon however, between the sixth and seventh decades, in the organ doors portraying the Evangelists (1557) in the church of Santa

J. Tintoretto, Self-portrait. Victoria and Albert Museum, London.

Maria del Giglio in Venice, in the "St. George and the Princess" in the National Gallery in London, in the "Piscina Probatica" in the church of San Rocco (1559), Tintoretto's language pours out in an imaginative excitement where the dramatic force of light, the catalyzing element of the chromatic and sketching values, emerges more and more. With an inner emotional and formal strength, based on luministic poetics, Tintoretto tackles the great religious and profane themes, always outside of any academic convention and completely independent of the other major painters in Venice in the second half of the 16th century: Titian, Paolo Veronese and Jacopo Bassano. If the presence of the workshop is nearly always noticeable in the commemorative canvases in the Palazzo Ducale, then in the religious works, for example the "Marriage in Cana" in the vestry of S. Maria della Salute (1561), the "Invention of the Cross" in Santa Maria Mater Domini, the new canvases in the Scuola di San Marco (1562/66) including the "Discovery of the Body of St. Mark" at the Brera Gallery in Milan, the enormous compositions of the "Adoration of the Golden Calf" and the "Last Judgement" (1562-65) in the church of the Madonna dell'Orto, he proudly works alone. Here, by means of a quick weaving of chiaroscuro, Tintoretto achieves a harmonious forceful magnificence of scenic conception pervaded by an existential restlessness, although he was firmly anchored, within the limits of the new intentions of the Catholic reform, to deeply religious thoughts made intelligible in a moving and poetic way to everybody by the simple and spontaneous representation of the story. In this way he perfigured the extraordinary pages of the Scuola Grande di San Rocco begun in 1564 and where the artist had the chance to assert his great visionary strength together with his intense capacity for work with conscious perfection.

Overall view of the Sala dell'Albergo.

In order to understand better Jacopo Tintoretto's poetic fantasies between 1574 and 1587 it is advisable to view the canvases starting in the Sala dell'Albergo (1564-1567), then proceeding to the Upper Hall (1570-1581) and finally descending to the Ground Floor Hall (1582-1587).

SALA DELL'ALBERGO (Hall of the Hostel)

On the 24 July 1546 the decision was taken to give the Guardian Grande of the Scuola di San Rocco the authority to have the walls of the Sala dell'Albergo decorated "with canvases or canevazze portraying figures, as he thinks fit and where he is advised, and the rest with paintings". This decision was not put into practice and a few years later, on 21 September 1553 Titian offered to undertake the large canvas to be placed on the wall behind the seats of the members of the Banca. Nothing came of the proposal however, although it was initially accepted unanimously. Only on 3 January 1557 was the decision taken to proceed with the permanent decoration of the Hall. For this purpose the Scuola set aside annually two hundred ducats. Nevertheless it was not until 22 May 1564 that this decision was put into effect with the promise on the part of the thirty six councillors to shoulder the expense of the first painting, the central canvas on the ceiling. It is significant that during the meeting one of the councillors, a certain Zani de Zignioni, declared himself ready to donate fifteen ducats on the understanding that the work should not be assigned to Jacopo Tintoretto. However it was in fact Tintoretto who, with self-confident resolution, secured the commission by presenting the finished central oval canvas representing the "Glorification of St. Roch" instead of the sketch asked for by the governors of the Scuola. In a meeting on 31 May 1564 the latter had decided on a competition in which some of the most reknown painters active in Venice were invited to take part and, according to Ridolfi (1648), they were: Andrea Schiavone, Federico Zuccari, Giuseppe Salviati and Paolo Veronese. After donating the canvas of the "Glorification of St. Roch" on 22 June 1564, not without some opposition, Tintoretto carried out without payment the decoration of the rest of the ceiling during the Summer and Autumn. On 22 July of the same year the gilding of the wooden part of the ceiling had begun and still was not finished by the following 22 October. In 1565, the year when Girolamo Rota was Guardian Grande, Tintoretto, now a brother of the school, started and finished the enormous "Crucifixion", placed exactly where Titian had offered to put one of his paintings in 1553. The following year, on 31 March, the governors of the Scuola decided to finish the decoration of the walls of the Sala dell'Albergo. They had Tintoretto paint three more canvases representing themes relating to the Passion of Christ. Tintoretto waited all through 1566 and the first months of 1567 before starting the work as he was busy since the May of that year painting the two canvases in the presbytery of the church of San Rocco and which he finished the following September (R. Pallucchini – P. Rossi, Tintoretto – the Religious and Profane works, Milan, 1982). In a little more than two years Tintoretto finished the decoration of the Sala dell'Albergo, so beginning in the Scuola Grande di San Rocco, in agreement with the majority of the clients as regards ideas and artistic intentions, an extraordinary and fascinating undertaking which was destined to last for the greater part of his whole career and to remain a living testimony of his art which was carried to such a point as to be recognized in popular thoughts and feelings through pictorial innovations of a both suggestive and inspired spontaneity.

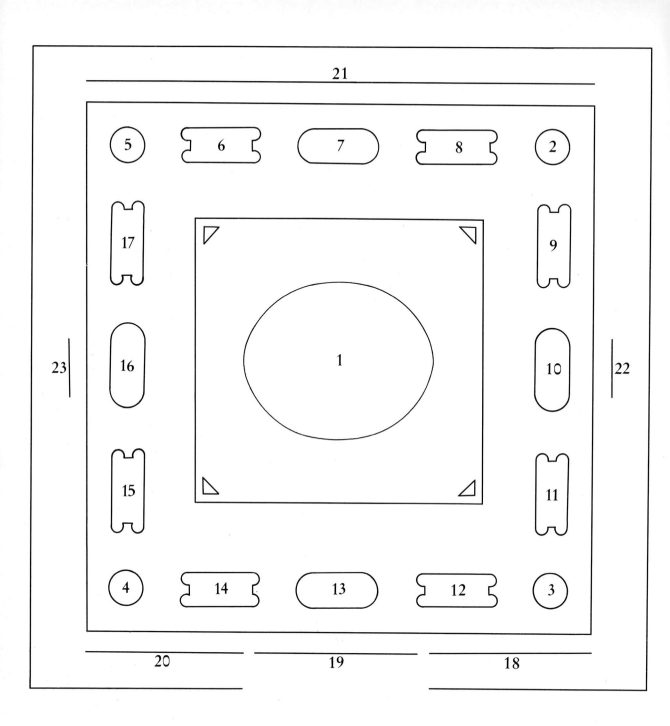

Plan of the ceiling and walls of the Sala dell'Albergo.

1) *The Glorification of St. Roch.* Oil on canvas (240×360) - June 1564

This great oval, in the centre of the magnificent carved and gilded ceiling, is the painting that Jacopo Tintoretto, according to the testimony in 1568 of Giorgio Vasari based on precise information gained during his stay in Venice in 1566, placed in the centre of the ceiling of the Sala dell'Albergo on 22 June 1564. He did not present a drawing of the work as had been asked for in the competition published by the Council of the Scuola di San Rocco on 31 May 1564. The other participants were Giuseppe Salviati, Paolo Veronese, Federico Zuccaro and Andrea Schiavone. In this way Tintoretto took the clients and the other participants by surprise, creating a great stir in Venetian artistic circles and resentment among the governors of the Scuola. To the latter, angry with the artist because «they had asked for drawings and not commissioned the work», Tintoretto, according to Vasari's story, «replied that that was his way of drawing, that he did not know how to work otherwise and that drawings and models had to be done that way so as not to deceive anybody and finally if they did not want to pay him for the work and his time and trouble, he would give it to them; and so speaking, although there was much opposition, he saw to it that the work even today remains in the same place». The donation of the painting by Tintoretto dates back to 22 June 1564 and the following 29 June the Brotherhood declared the competition null and void. In this oval Tintoretto shows his accomplished technique of composition, acquired by this time in numerous, analogous undertakings, by creating the figures of San Rocco, of the Eternal Father and of the Angels from a bold perspective worm's -eye-view and with skilful and vigorous strength. Above all the figure of the precipitating Eternal Father brings to mind, in its mighty three dimensional composition, Michelangelo's ideas and perhaps, as Schulz suggests (Venetian Painted Ceilings of the Renaissance, Berkeley-Los Angeles, 1968) is indirectly influenced by the frescoes in the style of Michelangelo by Pordenone on the dome of the church of San Rocco, now unfortunately lost. By not abandoning this repertoire of lightening foreshortenings, of steep perspectives, of contrasting colour combinations, Jacopo Tintoretto, in the harmonious brightness of the colours woven in elegant changing variations, seems to want to prove his ability to offer examples of decorations no less splendid than those with which Paolo Veronese, the new star of the Venetian pictorial scene, became established.

2) *Spring*. Oil on canvas (diam. 90) - ca. 1564.   3) *Summer*. Oil on canvas (diam. 90) - ca. 1564

4) *Autumn*. Oil on canvas (diam. 90) - ca. 1564. 5) *Winter*. Oil on canvas (diam. 90) - ca. 1564.

In 1564 around the central oval, in the golden splendour of the elaborate wooden frames, in an illusionistic decorative game which greatly recalls the examples of Venetian Mannerist ceilings by Giorgio Vasari (Corner-Spinelli palace, 1542), by Giuseppe Salviati (Santo Spirito in Isola today at the Salute, 1548 c.) and by Paolo Veronese (Vestry of the church of San Sebastiano, 1555), Jacopo Tintoretto inserts twenty canvases of varying sizes potraying "Cherubs' heads", "The Seasons", "Allegories of the Scuole Grandi of Venice", "The Virtues". These too were donated to the Scuola and according to De Tolnay (The interpretation of the pictorical cycles of Tintoretto in the Scuola di San Rocco, in "Critica d'Arte", 1960) "take the programme of the decoration (of the ceiling of the Sala dell'Albergo) from the religious moral plane (represented by the Allegories of the Scuola and by the Virtues) to the cosmic plane". As he had already done on the ceiling of the Square Hall in the Palazzo Ducale, carried out more or less at the same time (1564-65) as the one in San Rocco, Tintoretto represents in the four seasons by the same number of cherubs vivaciously set out in a flowing agility of poses in the middle of varying vegetations.

6) *Allegory of the Scuola di San Giovanni Evangelista.*
Oil on canvas (90×190) - ca. 1564.

These and the other allegorical figures of the Scuole Grandi and the Cardinal Virtues, portrayed in forced and artificial poses and attitudes of truly Mannerist origin, were particularly studied by Tintoretto in preliminary drawings. These remain some of the greatest examples of his graphic art and are some of the most significant for understanding the attraction he felt towards the Tuscan-Roman culture, in particular for the Michelangelesque style. It is this influence that takes him away from the Venetian drawing tradition. In the "Allegory of the Scuola di San Giovanni Evangelista" the eagle looms over the figure of the Saint who is leaning back and engrossed in reading. In the one of the "Scuola della Misericordia" the Virgin, who has inserted on her breast a medallion showing the Child Jesus, stretches out her arms drawing the brothers close to her. In the "Allegory of the Scuola di San Marco" the Saint lies opposite Saint John Evangelist and like the latter dedicates himself to reading.

7) *Allegory of the Scuola della Misericordia.*
Oil on canvas (90×190) - ca. 1564.

8) *Allegory of the Scuola di San Marco.*
Oil on canvas (90×190) - ca. 1564.

9) *Truth*.
   Oil on canvas (90×190) - ca. 1564.

10) *Allegory of the Scuola di San Teodoro*.
    Oil on canvas (90×190) - ca. 1564.

11) *Faith*.
    Oil on canvas (90×190) - ca. 1564.

In these three Allegories as well, the perspective-illusionistic effect presents the figures in formal solutions of flowing complexity. "Truth" twists her bust and every part of her body seems to spread out in the chromatic and luministic context. In the "Allegory of the Scuola di San Teodoro", identified as such by the writing on the preliminary drawing which is in the Drawings Room of the Uffizi in Florence, the warrior Saint seems to be barely contained in the oval where he stands out in the flashing light of his shining armour. The bended knee pose of "Faith", easily recognizable by the chalice held in her left hand, greatly recalls "Patience" by Giorgio Vasari, already part of a ceiling in Palazzo Corner-Spinelli in Venice.

The two female figures next to "Happiness" still have not been given a precise identification. Arranged in gestures of devote piety, they seem to pass through the clouds driven by a raging wind. Their robes of white and red lake billow out in violent swirls which are given prominence by shining threads of light painted with skilful vividness. The strength of their postures calms down into far more appeased symbolic rhythms in the splendid figure of "Happiness", the allegory recognized as such by the writing on the preliminary drawing in the Drawings Room of the Uffizi in Florence. While the legs are bent, following an idea by Vasari, as in "Faith" (cf. page 18), the bust is turned towards the front in a clear harmony of dark green and bright red.

12) *Female figure.*
Oil on canvas (90×190) - ca. 1564.

13) *Happiness.*
Oil on canvas (90×190) - ca. 1564.

14) *Female figure.*
Oil on canvas (90×190) - ca. 1564.

19

15) *Goodness*.
Oil on canvas (90×190) - ca. 1564.

16) *Allegory of the Scuola della Carità.*
Oil on canvas (90×190)) - ca. 1564.

17) *Generosity*.
Oil on canvas (90×190) - ca. 1564.

In the Drawings Room of the Uffizi in Florence there is also a preliminary drawing with writing on it for "Goodness". This permits an exact identification of the iconography of the allegory. The figure seems to draw back in a gesture of trusting piety while the legs, holding the large volume, stretch out along the edge of the oval. Portrayed in a far more complex movement, the allegory of the Scuola della Carità passes rapidly in a tangle of robes between light and shade, taking with her the two infants in an affectionate embrace. In a similar creation of movement a female figure is potrayed in flight, her arms open in a gesture of silent adoration and it is here that some have wished to identify the Allegory of Generosity. In every image on the ceiling Tintoretto's limitless imagination skilfully sets its seal on a decorative whole of unforgettable vividness.

Three apples. Oil on canvas (58×25) - ca. 1564.

This is just a fragment of the frieze with the coats of arms of the Scuole Grandi among cherubs bearing garlands of fruit and flowers and which runs along all sides of the Hall under the impost of the wooden frame of the ceiling. This fragment, found folded under another part of the frieze during restoration work in 1905, illustrates the flowing and sharp spontaneity of Tintoretto's brush-work in the vivid intensity of the polychromy which still remains intact. The various pigments have not been altered by the decolourizing effect of the light as has happened not only to the other parts of the frieze but also to the large canvases, above all in the upper Hall (cf. page 41).

Christ before Pilate (detail).

◀20) *Christ before Pilate*. Oil on canvas (515×380) - ca. 1566/67

After having finished the "Crucifixion" in 1565 (pages 28-29), Jacopo Tintoretto began the other canvases on the walls of the Sala dell'Albergo in 1566. These portrayed other important moments from the Passion of Christ and he finished them during the early months of 1567. The most admired has always been "Christ before Pilate". Perhaps while painting it Tintoretto partially kept in mind one of the wood-engravings in the series of the Piccola Passione by Albrecht Dürer, evidence of the lasting spell held by German graphics of the first half of the 16th century over the imagination of the protagonists of Venetian mannerist interpretations. The dramatic staging of the scene is however completely original. A large part of the staging has a composite architectural content played off in the changing chiaroscuro which is also rich in half-lights and deep shadows, in violent reflections, in sudden bright patches, in exstatic starts. In a very fine and measured luministic web the figure of Christ, wrapped in a white mantle, stands out like a shining blade against the crowd and the architectural scenery. He is centred by a bright ray of light and stands tall in front of the hypocritically bureaucratic judge that is Pilate who is portrayed in red robes and as if sunk in shadows. Certainly taking up the idea of Carpaccio in his "Envoy of English ambassadors to the King of Brittany" which belongs to the series of Stories of St. Ursula originally in the Scuola of the same name and today in the Accademia Galleries, Tintoretto portrays the old segretary at the foot of Pilate's throne. He leans against a stool covered with a dark green cloth and with great diligent enthusiasm notes down every moment, every word spoken by the judge amid the murmurings of the pitiless crowd which obstinately clamours for the death of Christ. Without any pietistic shield the Evangelical scene rises up with extraordinary spontaneity to deliver the deeply exemplary message: the dignity of the Son of God in subordinating his own feelings to his moral duty towards mankind.

19) *The Crowning with Thorns*. Oil on canvas (260×390) - ca. 1566/67.

The message of Christian piety told by "Christ before Pilate" also pervades the other canvases of the series of the Passion. "The Crowning with Thorns" is cleverly inserted around the outline of the tympanum of the door and does not show the tumult of the crowd that characterizes the other scenes. In the centre of the composition Christ is seated regally on the steps against the shroud and portrays the martyrized piety of the flesh. The prominent figures of Pilate and the soldier act as human wings on the left and right, framing the sorrowful apparition and prolonging the vision for the onlookers beyond the edge of the painting. In the strong stream of light that comes from the left, the shades of colour brighten up and vary extraordinarily: the red of Pilate's robes and of the soldier's and of Christ's mantle; the steel grey streaked with luminous reflections of the armour; the dull white spotted with blood of the shroud; the pinky yellow of the flesh of Christ with his pathetically sad face.

The Crowning with Thorns, detail.

The Ascent to Calvary, detail.

◀ 18) *The Ascent to Calvary*. Oil on canvas (515×390) - ca. 1566/67.

This agitated scene is set along a route rising at an acute angle; the first side, reading from left to right, is in deep shadow against which the chromatic tones of white, red, green, blue, yellow-orange of the robes of the two theives and their escorts stand out vividly; the second part of the procession is done in full light against the sulphur-coloured sky streaked with pink. It opens up with the dominating soldier seen against the light in the foreground who is holding the rope tied around Christ's neck and it is closed by the brightly coloured group of pious women preceded by the soldier who lets the pale pink standard flutter in the wind. It is in this second half of the procession that De Tolnay (1960, op. cit.) sees the appearance of "a triumphal procession" where the human pain of Christ, extraordinarily portrayed in the bent figure, almost succumbing under the weight of the large wooden cross, yields to the intense dramatic spirit.

21) *The Crucifixion*. Oil on canvas (536×1224) - ca. 1565.

The series of the Passion painted by Tintoretto for the Sala dell'Albergo reaches its climax in the "Crucifixion" which rates as one of the greatest works of the very wide span of the artist's activity. This is an enormous painting that takes up the whole wall opposite the entrance and on the bottom left beside the right leg of the white charger,

bears the following words with the date of realization and the signature: M.D.LXV./TEMPORE. MAGNIFICI/
DOMINI HIERONIUM/ROTAE, ET COLLEGARVM/JACOBUS TINCTOREC/TVS FACEBAT.
This magnificent painting, for which Tintoretto was paid two hundred and fifty ducats on 9 March 1566, received
immediate acclaim from his contemporaries. Evidence of this comes not only in writings but also in many
engravings among which the first and most famous is the one done by Agostino Carracci for Cardinal Ferdinando

The Crucifixion, detail.

The Crucifixion, detail.

De Medici in 1582, that is to say when Tintoretto was still alive, and in the enthusuastic study of the great protagonists of painting in the 17th century in Europe, such as Rubens and Van Dyck. Tintoretto prepared himself in depth to carry out this canvas. He made many preliminary drawings of the figures some examples of which still survive (Florence, Uffizi, Drawings Room; London, Victoria and Albert Museum; Rotterdam, Museum Boymans von Beuningen) and above all he sketched directly onto the canvas the extraordinarily detailed outline of the composition. This has been possible to verify, in this painting and in others by Tintoretto in

The Crucifixion, detail.

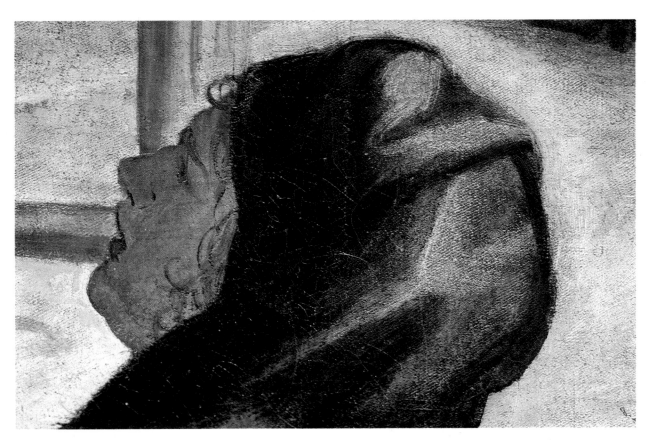

The Crucifixion, detail.

the Scuola di San Rocco, during the reinforcing carried out during the recent restoration (cf. page 8 and F. Valcanover, Review of: P. Rossi, The Drawings by Jacopo Tintoretto, Florence, 1975, in "Arte Veneta", 1976). The magnificent human setting, spread out horizontally, has its pivot in the crucified Christ who, in tragic solitude against the sky leaden with storm clouds, dominates and towers steeply above the group of mourners at the foot of the cross and above the crowd clamouring freely in groups precisely placed, like the rays of the sun, at the sides of the ladders, of the ropes and of the crosses of the theives. The tone-colour vividness that characterized "The Glorification of St. Roch" (cf. page 15) is subdued and the chiaroscuro bestows on the whole composition a fathomless spatial-perspective depth and makes the groups of horsemen at the sides, the crucified Christ, the mourners at the foot of the cross all emerge as solidly modelled into real space. The chiaroscuro also outlines with increasing swiftness of luministic effects the crowd as it moves away from the proscenium and then evokes it in the background as glowing streaks that intersect each other and mix together with the sparse elements of a devastated landscape, swept by the wind. Under the dynamic beating of the vivid and changing light, the chromatic keyboard throws out tonalities, harmonies, transformations first dense and hot, then pale and cold, which reach the peak of emotion in the group of mourners gathered at the foot of the cross. Here a group of heads bent over the Virgin's face, drawn with grief, stand out; especially beautiful is the profile of St. John Evangelist stretched upwards in silent adoration and the head of the woman, whose profile is lost, intent on catching a last breath of life from the Son of God.

In the scene which is extraordinarily well harmonized in spatial-luministic effect, the colours and light quiver intensely. In the yellowish, forcefully illuminated opening the final destiny of the two chance companions of Christ in torment is being enacted; meanwhile the spectators seem to shift in continual swirling movements, in concentric circles, which immediately involve external onlookers physically. The historical reality of the event is in this way surpassed by Tintoretto's fantasy which puts together a religious spectacle of harmonious magnificence, of poetic interpretation of the Christian miracle in which everyone must take part as participating and deeply touched actors because of the deep emotional charge. The artist himself is an example; he is portrayed bearded and leaning on a well-built stone bank above the figure of a labourer engrossed in hoeing the ground, and he is transfixed in silent contemplation of Mary and the mourners who close in around her.

The Crucifixion, detail.

22) *Prophet.*
    Oil on canvas (260,5×106) - ca. 1566/67.

23) *Prophet.*
    Oil on canvas (260,5×135,8) - ca. 1566/67

The two figures of the prophets, certainly not comparable in quality to the other paintings in the Sala dell'Albergo and therefore probably done by members of the workshop, are very damaged and for De Tolnay (1960, op. cit.) they are just spectators meditating in front of the "visions" expressed in the pictorial array. They are, for example, visitors to the room. You can see in fact how the Prophet on the right is looking towards the "Crucifixion" and the other one towards the paintings on the wall where one enters the room.

TIZIANO VECELLIO, *Christ carrying the cross*. Oil on canvas (68.2×88.3) - ca. 1506.

Perhaps already in 1508 when the church of San Rocco was finished and opened to the public the figure of "Christ carrying the cross" was worshipped there. It was very soon an unending, plentiful source of lavish charitable donations by the faithful destined for the ever increasing economic fortunes of the church and the Scuola Grande di San Rocco. The painting, as an engraving dated 1520 records, was housed in a marble tabernacle crowned by a lunette portraying the Eternal Father giving the blessing, the Holy Spirit and cherubs with expressions of spiritual anguish. Only in 1955 the canvas, long since removed from its original position and placed above the altar in the left apsidal chapel of the church of San Rocco, was transferred to the Sala dell'Albergo of the Scuola to make room for an altar-piece by Felice Carena dedicated to Pio X.

The attribution of the work is still very much in discussion. Numerous copies, even in the 16th century, testify to its quick rise to fame. While some scholars maintain that it is the work of Giorgione as indicated by Vasari in the 1550 edition of Vite, others favour Titian to whom the Tuscan writer attributes the work in the 1568 edition of the same Vite, specifying that the painting "… was thought by many to be done by the hand of Giorgione". Even if it is erased and has evident retouches in places, the original pictorial material proves to be of a thinness of pigment which can be found in the "Old Woman" by Giorgione in the Accademia Galleries and also in the "Concert" by Titian in Palazzo Pitti in Florence. The poetic thought behind the work, emerging in the intense dramatic force in which the contrasting souls of the two main figures are worked out, does not appear to be at all Titianesque: the scoundrel who haughtily stares at Christ who in his turn moves his pathetic face towards the onlooker. "Christ carrying the cross" in San Rocco could very well be one of the first works by Titian because of a certain timidity of composition in linking the two side figures, which are vaguely Leonardnesque, with the strong central group and because of the still very clouded pictorial technique. It was with works such as this that Titian made his debut on the Venetian pictorial scene at the beginning of the second half of the first decade of the 16th century as he tried, as sources recount, to master the technique and ideas of Giorgione.

SCHOOL OF GIORGIONE, *Christ in devotion*. Oil on canvas (55×81) - 1510 c.

This painting as well of Christ in devotion, which bears the letters YHS at the top left and XPS on the right, is varyingly attributed to Giorgione and to Titian. The most plausible proposal is however put forward by Pignatti (Giorgione, Venice 1969 and 1978) who considers the canvas to belong to the sphere of Giorgione "being close to the last works" (by the master of Castelfranco), such as the "Shepherd" in Hampton Court, that is to say towards 1510. The small canvas certainly seems to belong to the sphere of deeply lyrical and intimistic feeling of Giorgione who always expresses himself in the suspended concentration of the figure even when, at the end of the first decade of the 16th century, he seems to shows traces of the deeply psychological and colour expressiveness soon acquired from Titian.

Overall view of the Upper Hall.

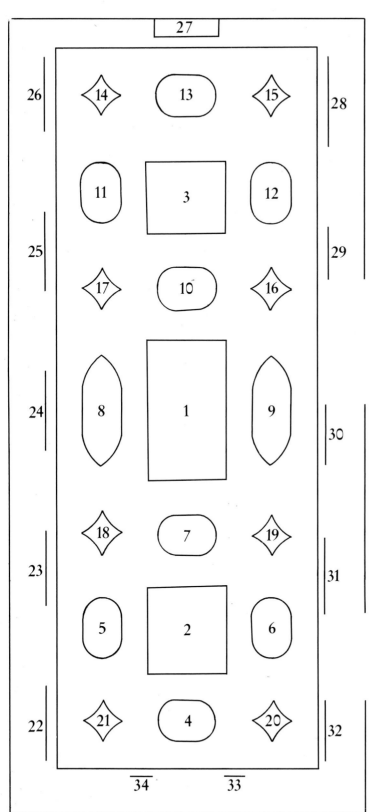

Plan of the ceiling and walls of the Upper Hall.

UPPER HALL

Ten years had hardly passed since the pictorial decoration of the Sala dell'Albergo was finished when Jacopo Tintoretto was already busy decorating the Upper Hall. The vast room was decorated with "canevazzi", paintings usually hired from year to year to adorn the Hall in occasion of the Patron's feast-day but which the Scuola di San Rocco had decided to buy on 24 August 1542: "to adorn this Hall until a further decision is made". On 9 July 1559 it was noted that time had made the "canevazzi" become decrepid and it was therefore necessary to carry out a new, worthier decoration. On 6 May 1574 the decision was taken to proceed with the re-decoration of the ceiling. The carpentery work was finished and the gilding still going on when on 2 July 1575 Jacopo Tintoretto proposed to carry out free of charge the large central square of the ceiling, promising to finish it by 16 August 1576, San Rocco's feast-day. Only a few months after finishing the no mean task of "The Brazen Serpent", on 13 January 1577 Tintoretto offered to paint the other two main ceiling paintings, asking only to be reimbursed for the cost of materials and colours, and letting the Banca and Zonta decide how much his work was worth. His conditions were immediately accepted by the Scuola, and just seven days later on 20 January, the artist began the two paintings: "The Miracle of Manna" and "Moses Drawing Water from the Rock". This work was still not completed when on 25 March 1577 Jacopo Tintoretto declared himself ready to paint the whole ceiling on the same conditions stipulated on the previous 13 January. This second offer was also accepted and a declaration made on 27 November 1577 by Tintoretto himself shows that by then the undertaking was at a satisfactory stage. The artist also declared that he was ready to dedicate his work for the rest of his life to the decoration of the Scuola, carrying out ten paintings, the altar-piece in the Upper Hall, the canvases for the new ceiling designed for the church of San Rocco and any other painting for the Scuola and the Church. Furthermore he promised to deliver three large finished paintings every year on San Rocco's feast-day. He himself would provide the colours but he asked for an annual allowance of one hundred ducats for the rest of his life should he fall ill after finishing he works in the Upper Hall. Tintoretto's proposal was accepted by the General Chapter of the Scuola on 2 December 1577. On 24 February 1578 the Scuola elected a commission made up of three Brothers who had the task of examining, judging and approving the paintings carried out by Tintoretto under his conditions. Both the artist and the clients kept to the agreement and the magnificent pictorial undertaking in the Upper Hall was finished in the Summer of 1581. In this Hall and in the Ground Floor Hall Jacopo Tintoretto gives of his best, leaving more or less to the workshop the work on the canvases commemorating Venice's fortunes in the large receiving rooms in the Palazzo Ducale. In the Upper Hall in particular, he carries the feeling of religious fervour, so ardently expressed in the Sala dell'Albergo, to a magnificence of conception and to an imposingness of forms which renew themselves in the continuous inventive onrush of meanings which are as intensely authentic as they are openly spectacular.

The Brazen Serpent, detail.

◀ *1)   The Brazen Serpent.* Oil on canvas (840×520) - ca. 1575/76.

This is the first painting on the ceiling of the Upper Hall carried out by Jacopo Tintoretto between 2 July 1575 and 16 August 1576. As De Tolnay correctly points out no exact iconographical programme was made beforehand as maintained by Thode (Tintoretto, Kritische Studien uber des Meisters Werke, in "Repertorium fur Kuntwissenschaft", XXVII, 1904) because, in the document dated July 1575 (cfr. page 41), Tintoretto proposed to paint the main canvas of the ceiling with a theme which he had mentioned orally or with another one more to the liking of the Guardian Grande of the Scuola. On the other hand, as De Tolnay points out, in "The Brazen Serpent" there already exists the guiding thread as to what will be the true theme of the other canvases on the ceiling and the walls of the upper Hall. In fact they reflect a theme based on interaction between the Old and New Testaments and the charitable aims of the Brotherhood of San Rocco: "The salvation and healing of the suffering humanity through a miracle of the Old Testament which is a forerunner of the Redemption of mankind through the sacrifice of Christ on the cross». The allusion to the healing of the sick by the Scuola is clear in the brazen serpent with a fish's head, twisted around the cross. The painting also visibly explains the passage from St. John's Gospel on the relationship between the subject-matter of the Old Testament and the redemption of mankind through the Crucifixion of Christ: "And as Moses lifted up the serpent in the wilderness, even so must the Son of man be lifted up: that whosoever believeth in him should not perish but have eternal life" (John III, 14-15). This portrayal is overwhelmingly dramatic. The turmoil of angels, following the Eternal Father emerging from the shadow, seems to force its way into the tangle of humans and serpents, while on the left, in the distance on a hill, Moses indicates the cross with the brazen serpent. The Michelangelesque magnificence of the concept and the strong plastic prominence of the forms turn out to be of an extraordinary and fascinating illustrative clearness, understandable by everyone in its content of Christian piety and human comfort, above all for his contemporaries who from April 1576 experienced the horrors of one of the most awful plagues ever to strike Venice.

2) *Moses drawing Water from the Rock*. Oil on canvas (550×520) - ca. 1577.

After finishing the central canvas on the ceiling of the Upper Hall Jacopo Tintoretto immediately began to carry out the two large side paintings at the beginning of 1577. In this painting, which clearly alludes to the task of the Brothers of the Scuola of quenching the thirst of the poor, De Tolnay (1960, op. cit.) sees that Moses, by his

Moses drawing Water from the Rock, detail.

clothes and pose, recalls the figure of Christ and that the water gushing from the rock symbolizes the blood that flows from the side of the Son of God. In one of his recent interpretations (Tintoretto at San Rocco. Historic-artistic research in occasion of the V centenary of the Scuola, Milan, 1980) Perocco however recognizes in the water that sprouts from the rock a forerunner of grace.

This episode which also comes from the Old Testament, so dear to the Middle Ages and the Renaissance, takes on a new and unforgettable form in the visionary imagination of Tintoretto, no less so than in the enormous "Brazen Serpent". Light decisively has the main role, even more so than in the latter painting. Every other formal value is subjected to it in a fantastic fervour and is reproposed in a continual breaking-down and rebuilding in effects of magnificent scenography. The focal point of the composition, placed to one side of the scene, is Moses who miraculously makes the water come out of the rock in the desert by striking the rock with a rod. The episode is introduced on the right by the incumbent figure of God astride a storm cloud inside an air bubble. Underneath, in the background, the vision of a camp rapidly crossed by a warrior on horseback opens up. In the impassioned and pressing rhythm of the chiaroscuro tones, all the pictorial and drawing elements contribute in giving the vivid impression of an endless rotating movement. In the dilated and fathomless space, where the burning imagination of Jacopo Tintoretto projects the physical appearances of reality, Moses stands irremovable like the rock, centred between light and shadow in the red lake of his robe, under the crystal-clear jet of water.

3) *The Miracle of Manna*. Oil on canvas (550×520) - ca. 1577.

The allusion to the sacrifice of Christ through which salvation can be reached is also exemplary in the third great painting on the ceiling of the upper Hall. For De Tolnay (1960, op. cit.) the improvised canopy is "an allusion to the canopy in the Temple at Jerusalem and also to the tablecloth of the Last Supper". The manna which falls on the believers "in the form of white hosts" also refers to the Last Supper and at the same time is an explicit reference to one of the acts of charity carried out by the Scuola di San Rocco: relieving the hunger of the poor. Even if it is better defined and more balanced than the two previous large canvases because of the creation of the two size human wings, that is to say the man with a basket on the left and Moses on the right, the scene is animated in depth by the rapid changing of perspective levels of light and shadow until arriving at the striking apparitions of God over the canopy and under it of the hills brought alive by very bright figures. Once again Tintoretto's brush-work knows how to scale with masterly speed the near and far in the most imaginative expressiveness. The speed of creation and realization, which is a characteristic note of Tintoretto's art, has not always been appreciated. If it was not liked by some of the Brothers of the Scuola, steadfast opponents of the artist (cfr. page 13), it was not understood by Giorgio Vasari who in 1566 in front of the Last Judgement in the church of the Madonna dell'Orto expressed doubts about the presumed inaccuracy and irregularity of the drawing and about the speed with which the details were filled in. Such doubts often recur in criticism, even contemporary ones (R. Longhi, Viaticum for five centuries of Venetian painting, Florence 1946).

The Miracle of Manna, detail.

4) *The Fall of Man*. Oil on canvas (265×370) - ca. 1577/78.

Whereas De Tolnay (1960, op. cit.) interprets original sin as the cause of the every evil thing in man, Schulz (1968, op. cit.) sees in the subject-matter of the canvas an introduction to the theme of the whole pictorial decoration of the Hall based on salvation. As in the same subject-matter dealt with almost thirty years before in the large canvas in the Scuola of the Santissima Trinità and today in the Accademia Galleries, the figures of Adam and Eve revolve around a tree. The atmosphere of dramatic expectation in the canvas in the Accademia Galleries is substituted however in this version, by the dramatic awareness of the consequences of the forbidden act, created by the very intense and strong toning of the chiaroscuro and by the wild landscape in which the episode takes place.

5) *The Eternal Father appears to Moses*. Oil on canvas (370×265) - ca. 1577/78.

This and the other two ovals placed at the sides of the canvas portraying "Moses Drawing Water from the Rock" are iconologically closely connected with it. The moment when God appears to Moses to announce to him the news of the promised land is carried out with meditated Manneristic sharpness of the cadences tackled with figurative and spatial rhythms, and which are free and very much alive in the impassioned luministic context.

6) *The Pillar of Fire*. Oil on canvas (370×275) - ca. 1577/78.

As in the previous picture, the scene where Moses leads the Jewish people into the desert guided by a pillar of fire is closely related to the meaning of salvation expressed in the canvas with "Moses Drawing Water from the Rock" (cf. page 44). Most of the section is taken up by the figure of Moses, seen from behind, powerfully and toweringly positioned and rhythmically struck by shadow and by the bright light against the orange-red and grey of the sky in the background and the white of the crowd watching the miraculous apparition at the bottom.

7) *Jonah leaves the whale's belly*. Oil on canvas (265×370) - ca. 1577/78.

De Toinay (1960, op. cit.) sees in this section, considered to be an allusion to water being the bearer of new life, a clear reference to "Moses Drawing Water from the Rock" (cf. page 44) on the ceiling and to the "Baptism" (cf. page 63), to the "Piscina Probatica" (cf. page 84) and to the "Resurrection of Christ" (cf. page 67) portrayed in the large canvases on the walls. With extraordinary pictorial ardour Tintoretto catches the moment when Jonah comes out of the enormous jaws of the monstrous fish and suddenly finds himself before God. The scene turns out to have an amazing intensity of feeling for life because of the characteristic strength behind the brush-work and the contrasting succession of shades of colour.

8) *The Vision of Ezekiel*. Oil on canvas (660×265) - ca. 1577/78.

The biblical subject-matter of this great oval is, through its meaning, clearly connected to the "Resurrection of Christ" (cf. page 67) and to "The Brazen Serpent" (cf. page 43): Ezekiel, under the commanding gesture of the Father, watches while the human bones become recovered with flesh. The three figures of the Eternal Father, of Ezekiel and of the naked man, built up in schemes of strong figurative contrasts, seem to force the actual limits of the painting.

9) *Jacob's Ladder*. Oil on canvas (660×265) -
ca. 1577/78.

This biblical episode is correctly considered by De
Tolnay (1960, op. cit.) to be an allusion to the
"Resurrection" (cf. page 67) and to the "Ascension
of Christ" (cf. page 81) portrayed in the large canvases on the walls of the Upper Hall. The swift
vivid description of the ideal ladder created in the
most phantasmagorical upside down perspective is
extraordinarily evocative of the distance that separates Jacob down below, seen from behind against
the light, from the Eternal Father who appears
indistinct in the pink glows of the sky-blue highest
heaven.

10) *The Sacrifice of Isaac*. Oil on canvas (265×370) - ca. 1577/78.

De Tolnay (1960, op. cit.) sees in this biblical episode clear links with the divine action in the "Raising of Lazzarus" (cf. page 79) and with the suffered obedience of Christ in "Praying in the Garden" (cf. page 69). It is one of the most deeply thought out and skilfully done of the ovals. In its strongly marked context of shades, in the three dimensional strength of the forms and in the vivid and changing chiaroscuro web, one of the most memorable poses is captured for ever: the moment when Abraham is stopped by the Angel just when he is about to take the life of his son Isaac, thus obeying the will of God.

11) *Elisha multiplies the Bread*. Oil on canvas (370×265) - ca. 1577/78. ▶

This oval, through its subject-matter, has links with many other paintings in the upper Hall, all of them clearly alluding to the Eucharist and to the duty of the Brothers to feed the poor: "Elijah fed by the angel" (cf. page 57) and the "Passover" (cf. page 57) on the ceiling; the "Miracle of the loaves and fishes" (cf. page 77) and "The Last Supper" (cf. page 73) on the walls. Most of the oval is taken up with the figure of Elisha who is handing out bread and who towers over the Jews in the desert. Tintoretto's work has however been altered, especially in the background, by old restoration work done by Giuseppe Angeli (1777-78).

12) *Elijah fed by the Angel*. Oil on canvas (370×265) - ca. 1577/78.

"Elijah fed by the Angel" is another very memorable oval on the ceiling because of the complete skilfullness of invention and the lyrical capacity for colour expression. As though shot from a bow, the divine messenger falls hurtling down from the left towards Elijah who is sleeping on his side. In the imposingness of the two figures, contained with difficulty in the oval, the precious keyboard of hues and of coloured reflections gives the scene, set in a wooded nook, the very apt impression of resigned devotion to the will of God. The scene depicts exactly the passage in the Bible where the story tells of Elijah on the road to Horeb "And as he lay and slept under a juniper tree, behold, then an angel touched him, and said unto him, Arise and eat" (I Kings, XIX, 5). It evidently belongs to the group of paintings (cf. n. 11, 13, 26, 28) directly linked to the theme of the Eucharist.

13) *The Passover*. Oil on canvas (265×370) - ca. 1577/78

After recent restoration work which has freed it of very heavy coats of re-painting the picture, once believed in greater part not to be by Tintoretto, now seems to be certainly by him. It is particularly fascinating because of the surprising luministic approach which creates an unforgettable adherence to the theme.
This painting too, like the others in the Upper Hall (cf. n. 11, 12, 26, 28), clearly alludes to the Eucharist.

GIUSEPPE ANGELI: 14) *The Vision of St. Jeremiah*; 15) *Abraham and Melchizedek*; 16) *Elijah on the burning chariot*; 17) *Daniel saved by the Angel*. Oil on canvas (265×265 each one) - ca. 1777-1778.

To complement the themes portrayed in the main canvases on the ceiling of the Upper Hall, Tintoretto painted in tempera eight rhomboid sections in chiaroscuro with biblical subject-matter. For a long time believed to have been restored by Giuseppe Angeli, recent work (cf. page 8) has shown that the eight paintings by Tintoretto were radically substituted with others by Giuseppe Angeli in 1777/78. This substitution has also been proved by documents published by Paola Rossi (1977, op. cit.) according to which the Inquisitors of the Scuole Grandi ordered Angeli to carry out true copies of the tempera paintings by Tintoretto which were in very bad conditions.

GIUSEPPE ANGELi: 18) *Samson draws water from the donkey's jaw*; 19) *Samuel and Saul*; 20) *Moses saved from the waters*; 21) *The three children in the furnace*. Oil on canvas (265×265 each one) - ca. 1777-1778.

The receipt for these copies still exists. It was written on 12 January 1778 by Giuseppe Angeli and he refers explicitly to the eight sections "redone in oil" following the models "that had been painted by Tintoretto in tempera". In the eight rhomboid canvases the tones which characterize the rather affected picturesqueness of Angeli, gained under the teaching of Piazzetta, appear evident. Its lively chiaroscuro structure moves, in clear tones, onto a plane of delicate and academic figurative characterization.

The Adoration of the Shepherds, detail.

◀ 22) *The Adoration of the Shepherds.* Oil on canvas (542×455) - ca. 1578/81.

In the first canvas on the outside wall of the Upper Hall Tintoretto's ideas result in a new freedom of composition. In an open scenic illusionism, the shepherds below present their gifts with impassioned and joyous gestures. They are counterpointed by the light and shadow created by the brightness from outside; above, main and secondary figures taking part in the divine event take on attitudes of conscious, almost solemn participation and are dazzled by the light which streams through the cracks between the wooden beams of the humble barn. The two different spiritual moments are underlined also by the different colour quality: without breaking the continuity the lower part is continually struck by reverberations and reflections and at the same time carefully and realistically evokes the animals in the stall, the brightly coloured peacock, the humble tools; the upper part is calmer and more relaxed although the wide chromatic background painting is strengthened by sudden, flashing rays of light. The story and its meaning is clearly recognizable by everyone. Anna Pallucchini (Tintoretto in the Scuola di San Rocco, Milan, 1965) correctly underlines the similarities between the painting by Tintoretto, dedicated in the Scuola di San Rocco as a good example to the humble people struck by particularly cruel ills, and a certain mysticism which was expressed in Venice in the second half of the 16th century by preachers among whom in particular Mattia Bellentani known for his "Practice of mental prayer" of 1573.
According to De Tolnay (1960, op. cit.) the painting must be considered in relation to the future liberation from sin as its placing near to the oval on the ceiling portraying the "Fall of Man" also leads us to believe (cf. page 48).

◀ 23) *The Baptism of Christ*. Oil on canvas (538×465) - ca. 1578/81.

The nearness of this canvas to the one portraying "The Adoration of the Shepherds" emphasizes the radical difference in ideas between the two paintings. Whereas in the "Adoration" the main moment of the event is shown off by a complex scenic and chromatic-luministic setting, in the "Baptism of Christ" it is given no particular importance. The two protagonists are banished to the left and evoked by the beam of light that strikes the back of the kneeling Christ whose face is sunk in shadows. John the Baptist is also immersed in the shadow as he bends forward in the act of pouring the water from the river Jordan over the head of the Son of God. Around the two main actors a wide open space is created. It is bounded on the right in the foreground by a steep rocky wing in whose deep shadow some spectators of Christ's baptism are undressing under the glance of the devout brother absorbed in prayer. On the left however, in the background beyond the river Jordan, those waiting for baptism throng together in a line. They are depicted in an extraordinary sparkling of blobs of colour and of luminous reflections. Evoked with astonishing rapidity of touch, the procession seems to extend on both sides, with no break in continuity, against the thick curtain of trees and under the blanket of heavy, threatening storm clouds. The quickly changing rhythms of light and the dense intermingling of figurative and spatial bonds create a sort of vortex in which the fantasy and emotion of the onlooker are immediately caught up. In front of this large canvas you become exactly aware how in the Scuola Grande di San Rocco Jacopo Tintoretto renews the most dear and traditional themes of religious iconography with a new freedom of creativity. He was driven by a popular faith which hardly feels the Pietistic effects of the order of the Counter-Reformation only a few years after the closure of the Council of Trent in 1563.

According to De Tolnay (1960, op. cit.) the large canvas relates to the neighbouring paintings on the ceiling, in particular to the one depicting "Moses Drawing Water from the Rock" (cf. page 44), because of the allusion to water being the source of life and freedom.

The Baptism of Christ, detail.

The Baptism of Christ, detail.

The Baptism of Christ, detail.

The Resurrection of Christ, detail.

◀ 24) *The Resurrection of Christ.* Oil on canvas (529×485) - ca. 1578/81.

In a dramatic crescendo the force of the chiaroscuro setting and of the web of composition concludes and centres on the arisen Christ. He is the invincible testimony of faith haloed by the divine dazzling light which blazes from the open tomb. His figure is splendidly characterized by the exuberant baroque eloquence of Boschini in 1660: "He stands unmoved, bright and resplendent / With more than golden rays all around". The four angels with large beating wings who have just removed the heavy marble slab from the tomb, are sort of inlaid into the supernatural light. At the same time two devout women come forward talking from the left deprived of natural light. The excitement of the divine event is underlined by the tones of the strong, bright colours brought together in contrasting harmonies in the shadows as well as in the heavily illuminated parts of the background. De Tolnay (1960, op. cit.) recalls how the theme of the canvas is pre-represented in the "Vision of Ezechiel" (cf. page 52) in the above oval on the ceiling.

25) *Christ praying in the Garden.* Oil on canvas (538×455) - ca. 1578/81.

With extraordinary mastery of light, of undescribable and spontaneous dramatic force, Tintoretto has emphasized in the night setting the important moments of this episode from the New Testament by bringing them all together. In the top right in the lonely spot in the garden Christ, in a red mantle and bent out of human suffering, receives the announcement of his imminent death from the divine messanger. The latter breaks in from the right in a bright reddish halo and his brightness creates reflections on the leaves of the shrubs. The same source of supernatural light highlights the two apostles fast asleep, the third only just awoken and the row of armed soldiers which can be glimpsed on the right advancing cautiously in the cold, still evening air to take the Son of God by surprise in the garden. In the course of Jacopo Tintoretto's work, and in particular in the canvases in the Scuola Grande di San Rocco, although altered in their intensity and colour combinations (cf. page 8), the luministic tension had always taken first place among his means of expression. In "Christ praying in the Garden" however it reaches one of its most mature and greatest moments. The human suffering of Christ has been caught by using endless figurative and temporal rhythms and with a spontaneous narrative vividness which immediately captures the emotion of the onlookers. It is a visionary interpretation that has been rightly compared to the one by El Greco: Christ absorbed in the tragic thought of death; the divine assurance of the angel who bears the bitter chalice; the fragile loyalty of the Apostles to their master; the deceitful furtiveness of Christ's persecutors so wonderfully expressed by the angry intermingling of their profiles brightened by dull, almost lunar whiteness. The burning intensity of Tintoretto's poetic imagination finds its most suitable means of expression in the rapidity with which it is carried out.

According to De Tolnay (1960, op. cit.) the subject-matter of the canvas is closely related to the "Sacrifice of Isaac" (cf. page 54) depicted in the oval on the ceiling. In both paintings in fact the focal point of emotion is the suffering caused by an undesired event enforced by the will of God.

Christ praying in the Garden, detail.

Christ praying in the Garden, detail.

Christ praying in the Garden, detail.

The Last Supper, detail.

◄ 26) *The Last Supper.* Oil on canvas (538×487) - ca. 1578/81.

No less than in the "Baptism of Christ" (cf. page 63) and in "Christ praying in the Garden" (cf. page 69) the scene of the "Last Supper" is represented by means of spatial and perspective bonds, fantastically enlarged. Tintoretto's capacity to always give a new, different interpretation to one of the best loved and most repeted themes of his figurative repertoire is remarkable. In the foreground two large figures of poor people at the sides of the restless dog are crouching on the steps. Beyond them the two-coloured check marble floor which rises towards the kitchen area in a steep and oblique perspective flight, is cut across diagonally from the right by the very long table against the shadowed wall which marks the limits of the rooms. Along the table the figures rapidly and proportionally get smaller. Every element in the composition comes together to create the effect of endless depth in the skilful luministic setting. The apostles are caught by two sources of light, one coming from the foreground and a second one which spreads from the passage in the background on the right, and they are highlighted by chiaroscuro in a tumult of spiritual poses and attitudes which spread along the table with vivid dramatic force only to quieten down in the figure of Christ. His is the smallest figure even though he is immediately recognizable by the dazzling halo. He has just aroused many emotions by introducing the sacrament of Holy Communion and by announcing his betrayal by one of the Apostles. Every image is defined with undescribable force by the increased, pressing rhythm with which the light breaks in from every side. In the description of the servants and serving-maids busy in the household store dominated by the great dresser and in the kitchen furnished with the large fireplace, the flowing brush-work renders the means of expression more immediate. Nevertheless nothing is lost of the truth of the physical and psychological aspects within the bright, chromatic settings, even if woven into the

The Last Supper, detail.

web of a memorative, powerful, transfiguring imagination. The deeply pictorial quality of the canvas did not go unobserved by Velasquez who made a copy while staying in Venice in 1649 to give to Philip IV and this copy is today kept in the Accademy of San Fernando in Madrid.

As De Tolnay (1960, op. cit.) points out, the sacrament of Holy Communion, the theme of the canvas, is also alluded to in the ceiling sections over the altar (cf. pages 54, 57, n. 11, 12, 13).

The Last Supper, detail.

◀28) *The Miracle of the Loaves and Fishes*. Oil on canvas (523×460) - ca. 1578/81.

In this canvas Tintoretto uses the same scenic structure as in the "Ascent to Calvary" (cf. page   ) carried out for the Sala dell'Albergo in 1566: a foreground in shadow against which a background in full light is diagonally set. In the dense half-shadow against the hill, that rises towards the left, the light shows up and outlines all the figures arranged in wide, curved poses. The figures waiting for the miracle to be performed cover the hilly area against a blue sky streaked by the first rosy light of sunset. The figures of Christ and Andrew are the focal point of attention as they encourage the boy with the basket to begin the miraculous distribution of the loaves and fishes. Every semblance of colour and light is arranged in a web of wide open spaces, of suggestive naturalness within a calm landscape.

This canvas too, like the previous one, is closely linked to the theme of the Eucharist.

The Miracle of the Loaves and Fishes, detail.

The Raising of Lazzarus, detail.

◀ 29) *The Raising of Lazzarus.* Oil on canvas (541×356) - ca. 1578/81.

As in the "Miracle of the loaves and fishes" the chiaroscuro structure seconds the cadenced and balanced contrast of figurative rhythms slowed down into poses and attitudes of studied harmony, as in the feelings of the main and secondary characters in this miraculous event. In the lower half enveloped in half-shadow Martha, the sister of Lazzarus who is plastically outlined by the thread of light, stretches out her arms and stares motionless and as if unbelieving at Christ who sits down calm and unmoved after pronouncing the life-giving words. She is outlined from behind and her lost profile makes her very beautiful. At the top, among the leafy branches of the trees clearly outlined against the glow of the sky mingled with pink and blue-grey light, Lazzarus, who is coming back to life, is freed from the bandages under the careful gaze of the crowd of spectators just made out beyond the small hill.
For the same miraculous ending to a cruel situation by divine providence; this canvas, like the one depicting "Christ praying in the Garden" (cf. page 69), is linked by its theme to the oval on the ceiling showing the "Sacrifice of Isaac" (cf. page 54).

30) *The Ascension*. Oil on canvas (538×325) - ca. 1578/81.

In this canvas, perhaps as in none other of the many paintings in the Scuola Grande di San Rocco, Tintoretto reaches an elevated point of lyrical poetry and of visionary imagination in his constant search for luministic effects without however diminishing or sacrifcing the vividness of the chromatic ranges in a naturalistic representation. Among the trembling and joyful mingling of angels' wings and of branches of olive and palm, Christ, the superhuman heroe, rises up with overwhelming vitality on the thick clouds of stormy cumulus, and he seems to cut through the upper edge of the painting. His sudden vigorous apparition advances dynamically towards the spectator because of the swirling unfolding of the chiaroscuro and the strong colour combinations. The towering apostle in the bottom left foreground, thrown backwards by the sudden apparition, seems to draw back towards his other companions grouped together around the table and around Moses and Elijah who are talking further off. The latter are skilfully highlighted on the yellowy tone of the plane brightened by yellow and pink rays of sun mixed with light and carried out with a flowing background painting technique. As in the "Resurrection" (cf. page 67) the poetic climate of the canvas is dominated by the figure of Christ flashing between light and shadow. His dramatic proportion in space is obtained through a melodramatic device that does not fall into banal theatricals. It recreates the moment of emotional suspense in the face of the miracle which is performed in the most spontaneous and understandable of ways for everyone, free of mistery and free of distress. With this capacity to strengthen the meanings of the figurative realizations so as to kindle and move the imagination and feelings of

The Ascension, detail.

The Ascension, detail.

even the most humble and simple people, Tintoretto reproposes the Christian legends in a previously unknown way and expresses in an uncomparable way his religious feeling of life.

According to De Tolnay (1960, op. cit.), the "Ascension" is prefigured by "Jacob's Ladder" (cf. page 53) depicted in the oval on the ceiling.

The Ascension, detail.

31) *La Probatica Piscina*. Oil on canvas (533×529) - ca. 1578/81.

This canvas is the least well preserved of all Jacopo Tintoretto's paintings in the Scuola Grande di San Rocco because of repeated restoration works long ago. Two of these were carried out in the 17th century: one by Domenico Tintoretto (1602) who redid the lower part from the young woman to the old woman turned towards Christ, and one by Lelio Bonetti (1696) (P. Rossi, 1971, op. cit.) and they were not removed during recent restoration work (1947) for methodological reasons. Nevertheless the setting of the scene is still admirable. It has a narrative wideness which compliments the meaning and harmony of the miraculous event. Under the thick curtain of a vine pergola, Christ, depicted in light and shadow on the right, bends over the paralysed man and frees him from all ills, while around the big pool of water the large crowd of sick people sit trustingly.

As De Tolnay (1960, op. cit.) points out, the theme of the canvas with its idea of water being the liberating force from ills and the source of life, is linked to the painting on the opposite wall depicting the "Baptism" (cf. page 63) and to the ovals above on the ceiling (cf. pages 44, 48, 51, n. 2, 5, 7).

La Probatica Piscina, detail.

◀ 32) *The Temptation of Christ.* Oil on canvas (539×330) - ca. 1578/81.

The scene is full of a particular, dramatic pathos because of the lively dialogue between Christ, who is seated at the top right under the rustic and disjointed roof, and the young handsome devil who breaks in from the bottom offering two fragrant loaves of bread. The clarity of the meaning of the episode – that is to say the urgency of the physical need of hunger – is accompanied by a splendid coloured web which reaches its peak in the tones of bright pink of the wings and of the mantle of the arrogant figure of the devil. According to De Tolnay (1960, op. cit.) the "Temptation" is prefigured on the ceiling by the oval depicting "The Fall of Man" (cf. page 48).

The Temptation of Christ, detail.

33) *St. Roch*.
   Oil on canvas (250×80) - ca. 1578/81.

34) *St. Sebastian*.
   Oil on canvas (250×80) - ca. 1578/81.

The strong formal structure of the two Saints is highlighted by the intensity of the light and the three dimensional chromatic and luministic tones. As De Tolnay (1960, op. cit.) suggests they really seem to be "kidnapped spectators", from the wall opposite the altar, of all that Jacopo Tintoretto has portrayed on the ceiling and along one wall of the Hall, which takes on the meaning of "School of the knowledge of God in a religious-aesthetic sense". The attribution of the work to Domenico Tintoretto by Eikemeier (Der Gonzaga-Zyklus des Tintoretto in der alten Pinakothek, in "Münchner Jahrbuch der Bildenden Kunst", 1969) has not been conferned by the recent restoration (1971).

27) *The Apparition of St. Roch.*
Oil on canvas (495×246) -
ca. 1588.

Dated 1588, just like the "Visitation" (cf. page 91) it was carried
out with a lot of help from collaborators as the 1967 restoration work
has shown. In particular Domenico
Tintoretto helped his father Jacopo
in the undertaking. The latter was
certainly the creator of the work
which is set in the almost cumbersome presence of St. Roch at the
top among the clouds where he
looms over his worshippers.

TIZIANO VECELLIO: *the Annunciation*. Oil on canvas (166×266) - ca. 1540.

The canvas was bought by the Scuola in 1555 through the testimentary legacy of the legal expert Amelio da Cortona, a member of the Brotherhood of San Rocco. Together with the "Visitation" by Tintoretto, it was originally placed over one of the arches of the landing of the main staircase which joins the Ground-Floor Hall to the Upper Hall of the Scuola. It was substituted in 1936 by the painting with "S. Girolamo", attributable to Leonardo Cosona, which was permanently lent by the Accademia Galleries.

Many critics attributed it in part to Titian's school and it was varyingly dated between 1526 and 1545. However after the recent restoration (1973) it showed such quality, both in conception and realization, that it can be attributed to Titian alone and dated around the year 1540. The angel in a confused tangle of white and red lake robes breaks in from the left, the hand raised in the gesture of the annunciation. Under the classical portico the Virgin seems almost belittled behind the wooden lectern, in a pose of resigned submission to the will of God. The intimate character of the apparition is underlined by the presence of everyday objects and animals: the quail, the fruit placed on the steps of the lectern, the half-open work basket.

The Visitation. Oil on canvas (158×237) - ca. 1588.

This canvas and the altar-piece (cf. page 89, n. 27) are mentioned in a receipt for 16 ducats signed by Jacopo Tintoretto on 15 May 1588. However in contrast to the "Apparition of San Rocco", the "Visitation", which was originally hung over an arch of the main staircase landing, is unquestionably by Tintoretto and well illustrates his extremely artistic work. It was substituted in 1936 by a "Virgin and Child and two camerlengos" of the Venetian school of the 16th century taken from the Accademia Galleries. The meeting between Mary and Elizabeth takes place under the affectionate and thoughtful gazes of St. Joseph on the left and St. Zacharias on the right. The intensity of this emotional moment is admirably created by the balanced suspension in space of poses and gestures through an emphasized perspective from below of the two towering female figures. They are depicted in robes of orange, of blue-green, of red and white as though sparkling against the dull grey flickering light of the very close horizon.

GIAMBATTISTA TIEPOLO: *Agar and Ishmael succoured by the Angel.* Oil on canvas (140×120) - ca. 1733.

This picture and the matching one depicting "Abraham visited by the Angels" were bought by the Scuola in 1785 and are two great moments in the art of Giambattista Tiepolo at the beginning of the fourth decade of the 18th century. This was immediately after the return of the artist from Milan where he painted frescoes in the Archinto and Casati-Dugnani palaces and when, under a renewed interest in Piazzetta's painting rich in dense brightness, he drafted the two masterpieces of the "Adoration of the Child" in the vestry of the Basilica of St. Mark's and the "Education of the Virgin" in the church of the Fava in Venice. In this canvas the images, very delicately drawn and coloured, appear with impetus in the foreground, thus creating a strong, lyrical, psychological emotion.

GIAMBATTISTA TIEPOLO: *Abraham visited by the Angels*. Oil on canvas (140×120) - ca. 1543.

The so strong and appropiate picturesqueness which characterizes the matching picture (cf. page 92) is no less in this canvas. The figure of Abraham praying stands out clearly in the brightness of the clouds and of the robes of the angel who furtively watches him from in front. The group of angels, so sensually done in the soft tenderness of their flesh and the richness of the tones of their silk robes, is one of the most memorable pieces of the radiant painting of Giambattista Tiepolo. It is exactly the small easel canvases like this one that illustrate the most creative and poetic moment of Tiepolo's art, even though his art attains the same level of creativity in all its extraordinary scenographic imagination in the large altar-pieces and in the magnificent decorative frescoes.

Portrait of a man. Oil on canvas (72×57) - ca. 1573.

This portrait of a mature man, captured in such a realistic position of deep devotion and dated 1573, has been thought to be one of the distinguished officials of the Scuola or indeed a self portrait of Tintoretto himself. This latter identification however has no serious links with the traditionally certain iconography of the great artist.

BERNARDO STROZZI: *San Rocco*. Oil on canvas (78×67) - ca. 1640.

Indicated by 18th century sources as being in the Saletta della Cancelleria, this small painting is representative of the picturesqueness of Bernardo Strozzi's work with its vivid chromatic effects developed from examples of Ruben's school. After arriving in Venice towards 1630 Strozzi, a Genoese, contributed together with Fretti and Liss in renewing the tired lagoonal painting of the first decade of the 17th century.

GIUSEPPE ANGELI: *San Rocco in glory*. Oil on canvas (251×166) - ca. 1754. *Faith*. Oil on canvas (155×150) - ca. 1754. *Charity*. Oil on canvas (155×150) - ca. 1754.

These three canvases decorate the Chancery ceiling of the Scuola and were commissioned from Giuseppe Angeli by the Guardian Grande Antonio Bianchi in 1754 and were finished before 18 September of the same year (P. Rossi, 1967, op. cit.). Even if a Tiepolesque moment of Angeli is reflected in the ease of composition, the three paintings still retain the characteristic soft, silvery range of colours of the follower of Piazzetta. This fits in so well with the 18th century richness of the stuccowork by Carpoforo Mazzetti Tencolla within which the paintings are inserted.

ANTONIO ZANCHI: *The Virgin appears to the plaque victims* (detail). Oil on canvas (555×335 and 705×635) - ca. 1666.

This is one of the most intense details of the great painting composed of two canvases divided only by a pilaster which, as the inscription on the bottom right of the larger canvas records, was finished by Antonio Zanchi on 14 October 1666. It was commissioned by Bernardo Briolo, the Guardian Grande. The enormous composition evokes the terrible plague of 1630 which caused so many bereavements among the Venetian popolation. Zanchi, the great Venetian naturalist painter of the 17th century, was inspired by the theme to create a severe and dramatic magnificence in his concept of composition and of pictorial content which shows traces of the visionary imagination of Tintoretto ever present in the Scuola.

PIETRO NEGRI: *The Madonna saves Venice from the plague of 1630* (detail). Oil on canvas (555×335 and 705×635) - ca. 1673.

These details are significant of the "shadowy" style, of the bold strength of the 17th century Pietro Negri who was brought up in the circle of the naturalistic paintings by Antonio Zanchi. The artist finished the work, which remembers the terrible plague of 1630 in Venice, on 20 August 1673. It was commissioned by the Guardian Grande of the Scuola Angelo Acquisti. The miraculous apparition of the Virgin, through St. Mark's intercession, takes place against the steaming background of Venice where the Basilica della Salute can be seen. The Basilica, begun in 1631 as votive thanks for the end of the plague, was only completed in 1687 but evidently by 1673 the most fundamental parts had been finished.

P. Negri, The Madonna saves Venice from the plague of 1630, detail.

GIROLAMO PELLEGRINI: *Charity with the torch of Religion in front of the poor and sick presented by San Rocco*. Fresco (512 diameter) - ca. 1700.

The fresco represents the highest point reached by Girolamo Pellegrini's smooth and luminous painting, by now unrelated to the naturalism of the "shadowy" style. In this way he attempted to strengthen the tradition of Paolo Veronese by bringing the decorative baroque Roman style to the examples by Pietro da Cortona to which the artist had the opportunity of dedicating himself in his early years.

Overall view of the Ground Floor Hall.

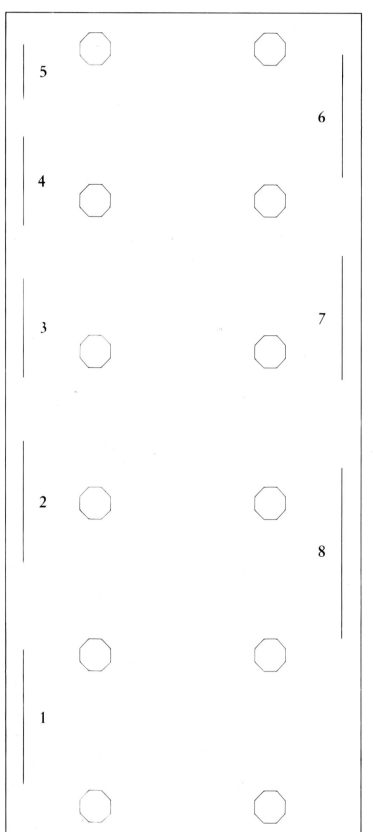

Plan of the walls of the Ground Floor Hall.

GROUND FLOOR HALL

After the completion in 1581 of the large canvases in the Upper Hall and the unfulfilled realization of the project for the decoration of the ceiling of the church of San Rocco, which he had declared himself ready to carry out on 27 November 1577, Jacopo Tintoretto found himself busy with many commissions, the most important being official ones in the most impressive rooms of the Palazzo Ducale. Nevertheless already in 1582 he started working again in the Scuola di San Rocco, dedicating himself to painting the canvases on the walls of the Ground Floor Hall. In fact there is a note relative to the cost of the frame for the "Adoration of the Magi" dated 16 July 1582. For the following years, from 1583 until 1587, further precise records, showing how the work was proceeding, exist. The last is dated 12 August 1587 and is a note of expenses from which it can be deducted that the "Circumcision" was the last painting to be placed in the Ground Floor Hall. However Tintoretto continued to receive the annual allowance of one hundred ducats agreed upon in the November of 1577. The last payment was made on 1 May 1594, that is to say not very long before the death of Jacopo Tintoretto on 31 of the same month. Out of the whole series of paintings in the Ground Floor Hall, only the "St. Mary Magdalen" and the "St. Mary of Egypt" are not mentioned in the documents of the Scuola and neither by the guides nor by 15th and 16th century sources. This omission, and because the two paintings fit in badly with the iconographical whole of the Hall, makes Tietze (Sketches by Jacopo Tintoretto in "Arte Veneta" 1951) think that these came from another place, being part of a group together with two male figures, one of which has been identified in a "Hermit in a wood" and whose sketch is still in the Museum of Historic Art in Princeton. Other scholars however maintain that the two extraordinary "Landscapes" belong to the original decoration of the Ground Floor Hall of the Scuola Grande di San Rocco and are representative of the Mariological meaning of the series, proved by the presence of the "Virgin Mary" (De Tolnay, 1960, op. cit.) where the miraculous element prevails (E. Huttinger, Die Bilderzyklen Tintorettos in der Scuola di San Rocco, Zurich, 1962). According to Niero (in "Venice and the plague 1348/1797", Venice 1979) the two figures of the Saints allude to the shameful diseases widespread during that century, such as lues or syphilis, which were considered a form of epidemic like the plague. However there seems to be no doubt that the two "nocturnal landscapes", conceived in such an imaginative way, are the natural conclusive stages to a formal procedure founded on very fervid sentimental motives and which finds its main means of expression in light.

In August 1587 the placing of the "Circumcision" in the Ground Floor Hall completed the decoration of the receiving rooms of the Scuola. Here Jacopo Tintoretto offers an uncomparable picture of his art through more than two decades of the last part of his creative career by means of the density and perfection of his imaginative inventiveness. The interaction between the unforgettable pages of Tintoretto and the Scuola Grande di San Rocco is such that nobody can think back to the first without evoking the second and viceversa remember the latter without associating it with the poetic strength of the former.

1) *The Annunciation*. Oil on canvas (422×545) - ca. 1582/87.

The announcement of the imminent divine maternity is given by the Angel to Mary in surroundings where everything is realistically described down to be the smallest detail: the delapidated brick base and column; the two-coloured floor of large marble tiles; the straw-bottomed chair which clearly shows the passing of time; the work basket and its contents at the Virgin's feet; in the background the large bed covered by a canopy. No less realistic, even if in a theatrically scenographic sense, is the outside setting where Joseph is busy with his work surrounded by carpenter's tools hung outside the hut. Such objective description of the surroundings is contrasted with the visionary intensity of the miraculous apparition of the heavenly messenger and the joyful evangelical song, which break in from the left. They are preceded by the Holy Spirit in the form of a snow-white dove with unfolded wings, almost perpendicularly above the Virgin's head. In the strong ink shadowing every image stands out strongly and takes on a spontaneous scenic emotiveness which immediately catches the attention of the onlooker. In the finished work weighed down by some details – the Virgin's head, the mantle of the Angel messenger, the flying cherubs – (R. Pallucchini – P. Rossi, 1982, op. cit.) the hand of Domenico Tintoretto, Jacopo's son, has been correctly recognized.

The Annunciation, detail.

2) *The Adoration of the Magi*. Oil on canvas (425×544) - ca. 1582.

It was completed in July 1582 and was therefore the first of the canvases of this series in the Ground Floor Hall to be carried out. The "Adoration of the Magi" shows the strength of Tintoretto's visionary gift to be unchanged. Taking advantage of the twilight hour he emphasizes the intensity of the luministic values. Above and along the brick walls and the wooden planks, the episode unfolds frontally under bright light which makes the physical and emotional gestures of the Wise Men stand out. Balthazar is beautiful, bending forward and wearing a turban that shines like a multicoloured jewel in the faint half-shadow. The harmonious night setting of the foreground gives way in the background on the right to the apparition of the procession of the Three Kings, broken up by traces of glowing light. The procession advances slowly from far-off lands guided by the star which has arrived directly above the Holy Child's head. In the carefully considered scheme of sudden flashes, of burning glows, of dim sparklings, the forms seem void of any three dimensional prominence and, having lost their body weight, they either flood over into surfaces filled with light or drown deeply where colour is not graduated in a tuneful tone-structure but is beaten out in separate notes within an almost arabesque whirling.

The Adoration of the Magi, detail.

The Adoration of the Magi, detail.

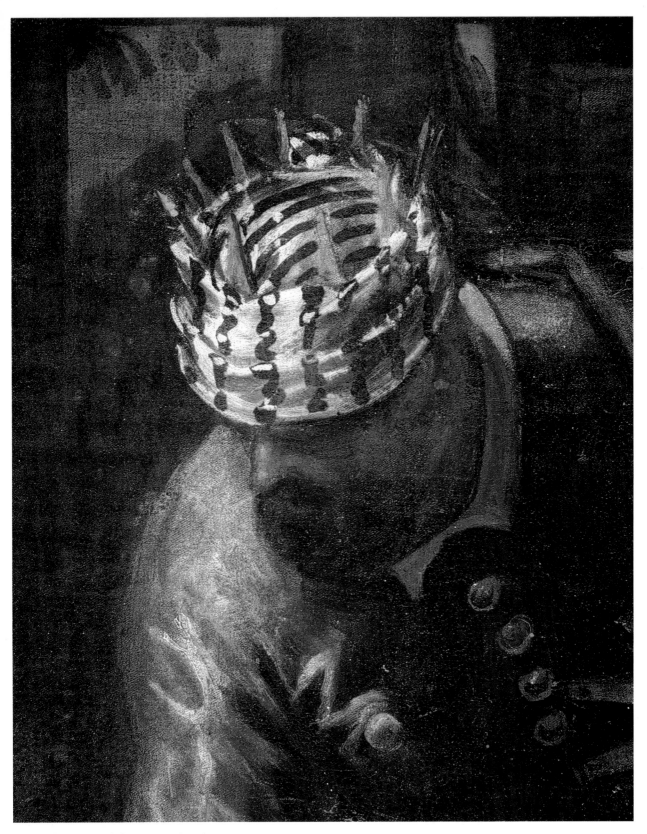

The Adoration of the Magi, detail.

3) *The Flight into Egypt.* Oil on canvas (422×580) - ca. 1582/87.

In the wooded hollow, after furtively avoiding every inhabitated place, Mary and Joseph together with the Holy Child, who have just escaped the genocide ordered by Herod, prepare to take a rest. Their feelings of fear and apprehension also pervade the wide landscape scenery lyrically described with a preoccupied emotional charge in the silent life of the fields, in the hills and in the snowy mountains which follow each other as far as the far-off horizon under the blue of the vast sky broken up by whitish clouds with pink reflections. The many beautiful details evoked within the density of the atmosphere of the hour that precedes twilight, are brought to an exemplary expressiveness of light, in its relentless breaking out in mysterious and agonizing flashes. On the left, in the foreground, in the web of dull greens, browns and whites of the landscape, the group of fugitives and their humble packs are depicted with concise reality in every element of form and colour. At the same time on the right the landscape scene, built up with extraordinary, quick brush-strokes and enlarged into fathomless depths, opens out. The waves on the pond, whipped up by the breeze, sparkle; the walls of the isolated cottage shiver in golden glows; the profiles of the tree trunks and branches are lit up by bright threads of light; the crests of the hills and the outlines of the mountains loose their composure in a myriad of fragments of light. In the poetic weaving of the chromatic material and of the luministic web, the painting reaches a cosmic plane, as it swells as if through internal pressure. The landscape ranks among the most memorable of Venetian and European art of all time because of the masterly graphic and chromatic creation with which the real theme is worked and transfigured by the imagination of Jacopo Tintoretto.

The Flight into Egypt, detail.

The Flight into Egypt, detail.

The Flight into Egypt, detail.

4) *The Slaughter of the Innocents*. Oil on canvas (422×546) - ca. 1582/87.

The atmosphere of preoccupation, only just touched on by a slight apprehension in the "Flight into Egypt" (cf. page 112), develops radically in the "Slaughter of the Innocents" where it becomes a tragic, violently dramatic pathos created by the unrestrained tangle of forms in the cruel scene. In the controlled melting-pot of light and shades, every figurative borrowing, although altered as already stated, from Michelangelo, from Raphael and from the Mannerist sculptors, in particular from Giambologna, is transfered and absorbed in a new image of Tintoretto's vision of harmonious dramatic force. Episodes of exceptional cruelty follow one after another in a zigzag, carried out with a memorably quick touch, in the overwhelming rhythm of flashing crosspieces of light through the shadows in an extraordinary quickening of every formal element. On the left a high wall blocks all means of escape; on the right in the background a portico can be glimpsed which opens onto a wooded landscape where the cruel massacre continues. All the details are of epic expressive violence and some attain high points of poetic effectiveness. For example the mother who in vain is trying to hold back the blade ready to pierce her son and the other one who agonizingly stretches forward from the wall in an attempt to reunite herself with her own already dead child. The individual episodes are however beautiful and augment in narrative effectiveness because they are amalgamated under the unifying, continuous force of radiant lights into a whole that gives off an inspiration of dramatic greatness beyond any scenic pretence. Once again Jacopo Tintoretto cleverly attains the result of lowering his own poetic thoughts into a spiritual expression where imagination and reality merge in the concreteness of a photogram in which every event is clearly justified for everybody in its deep religious and moral aims.

The Slaughter of the Innocents, detail.

The Slaughter of the Innocents, detail.

The Slaughter of the Innocents, detail.

St. Mary Magdalen, detail.

◀5) *St. Mary Magdalen.* Oil on canvas (425×209) - ca. 1582/87.

The increasingly taut and fascinating development of the luministic interpretation of reality in its poetic strength, clearly noticeable in the varying moments of Jacopo Tintoretto's art in the Scuola Grande di San Rocco, reaches a very high peak in "St. Mary Magdalen" and in "St. Mary of Egypt". St. Mary Magdalen is captured from the front, engrossed in reading, and given prominence like the large tree trunk on the left by a phosphorescent light falling on a magically mysterious nature. She is succintly defined in the final fleeting instant before the night shadows fall on the outline of the rustic cottages, on the rolling plains, on the ridges of the hills and mountains that make lines across the storm threatened sky pervaded by reddish shades. The magic brightness consumes the colour in a range of burnt, almost monochromatic hues, while the forms grow soft in a visionary, fleeting apparition of an intimate and imaginative interpretation of the true facts within a space of undefined and undefinable depth, which seems to swallow up in itself the onlookers by a magic spell.

◀ 6) *St. Mary of Egypt*. Oil on canvas (425×211) - ca. 1582/87.

No less than in the painting of Magdalen, the small silhouette of St. Mary of Egypt stands out by means of bright rays of light as an integrating element of the wide, open landscape. She takes part in its respite thick with the trembling shadows, with the countless reflections, with the reverberations, glows and luminous streaks of late evening. Looking up from her book, the Saint contemplates the landscape before her now made silvery by the moolinght on the water of the stream and on the outline of the high ground. The imaginative transformation of reality touches on a new, great poetic note in the silence of the feelings and in the motionless natural atmosphere, within unlimited perspective and spatial effects. In this way, almost at the end of the long road of human and artistic story, when he had already attained the most enchanting and basic form of light to give expression to his imaginative vision, Jacopo Tintoretto concludes the magnificent story begun more than twenty years before in 1564 in the Scuola Grande di San Rocco. He has always followed an impetuous and original vision, pervaded by a genuine and spontaneous religious feeling, as sincerely popular as alien to the devotional insistencies of the Counter-Reformation, in a sincere spiritual attitude and conscious of the worries and crises that afflicted his contemporaries.

St. Mary of Egypt, detail.

7) *The Circumcision*. Oil on canvas (440×482) - ca. 1587.

This is the last canvas painted for the Ground Floor Hall and it was placed in its actual position in August 1587. Recent restoration (1970) has confermed the ample participation of Jacopo Tintoretto's workshop in the painting, a fact already recognised by all the critics. This emphasizes how the creativity of Jacopo is distorted by the intervention of a collaborator both in the rather dull quality of the colour and in the heavier figurative results. Thus Jacopo Tintoretto's shining portrayal becomes humiliated into a prosaic descriptive slowness.

The Circumcision, detail.

8) *The Assumption of the Virgin*. Oil on canvas (425×587) - ca. 1582/87.

Recent restoration (1970) has not been able to completely put right the consequences of the many restorations undergone by the painting. The ones by Angelo Vidali in 1678 and by Antonio Florian in 1834 particularly stand out. Although the integrity of the pigments is altered, the work still shows the creative commitment and sentimental inventiveness of Jacopo Tintoretto and its direct application in his work. The Virgin rises up to heaven pushed by a sudden gust of wind which separates the postures of the apostles. Each one is caught in a particular emotional moment in front of the miraculous happening and is drawn in by numerous feelings: incredulity, marvel, estatic adoration. Their large semi-circle – and this is the part that most results poor in colour because of past unorthodox interventions – is contrasted with the bright and blazing circle that turns incessantly around the Virgin. On the right two old men, certainly portraits of Brothers of the Scuola, carefully watch what is happening between heaven and earth. Tintoretto portrayed them in the canvas to remember the extraordinary association, which had lasted over twenty years, between the artist and the governors of the Scuola Grande di San Rocco.

The Assumption of the Virgin, detail.

INDEX

BIBLIOGRAPHICAL NOTES

The bibliography on Jacopo Tintoretto's painting in the Scuola Grande di San Rocco is impressive. Only the detailed studies are mentioned here. They are: R. Berliner (Forschungen über die Tätigkeit Tintorettos in der Scuola di San Rocco, in "Kunstchronik", 1920); R. Pallucchini and M. Brunetti (Tintoretto a San Rocco, Venezia 1937); Ch. de Tolnay (L'interpretazione dei cicli storici del Tintoretto nella Scuola di San Rocco, in "Critica d'Arte, 1960); E. Hüttinger (Die Bilder zi Klen Tintorettos in der Scuola di San Rocco zu Venedig, Zürich, 1962); A. Pallucchini (Tintoretto alla Scuola di San Rocco, Milano, 1965); J. Schulz (Venetian painted ceilings of the Renaissance, Berkeley-Los Angeles, 1968); G. Perocco (La Scuola di San Rocco, Venezia, 1979 and Tintoretto in San Rocco. Historical-artistic research in occasion of the V centenary of the Scuola, Milano, 1980); and the most recent general treatises by T. Pignatti and VV.AA. (Le Scuola di Venezia, Milano, 1981) and, above all, by R. Pallucchini-P. Rossi (Tintoretto – Le opere sacre e profane, Milano, 1982).
To reconstruct the succession of events resulting from Jacopo Tintoretto's presence in the Scuola Grande di San Rocco, it is of course fundamental to study the documents in the possession of Venice's State Archives and of the Archives of the Scuola Grande di San Rocco. The first person to study these documents methodically was Berliner in 1920.

The details of Tintoretto's paintings, which are reproduced here, were chosen by the author in 1974 for a publication never published.

Photography: Giacomelli Venezia
Printed: May 1999

Cover Picture:
The Flight into Egypt, detail.